THE GREAT ADVENTURE

ROBERT LEWIS

LifeWay Press®
Nashville, Tennessee

Published by LifeWay Press®

Fifth printing 2009

ISBN 978-1-4158-2290-6
Item 001260515

Dewey decimal classification: 248.842
Subject headings: MEN\CHRISTIAN LIFE

Art direction: Jon Rodda
Design: Jay Smith, Juice Box Designs
Photography: cover, Steve Satushek/Getty Images; back cover, Punchstock

To order additional copies of this resource, write to LifeWay Church Resources Customer Service; One LifeWay Plaza; Nashville, TN 37234-0113; fax (615) 251-5933; phone toll free (800) 458-2772; e-mail *orderentry@lifeway.com;* order online at *www.lifeway.com;* or visit the LifeWay Christian Store serving you.

Printed in the United States of America

Leadership and Adult Publishing
LifeWay Church Resources
One LifeWay Plaza
Nashville, TN 37234-0175

TABLE OF CONTENTS

ABOUT THE AUTHOR

Robert Lewis is Pastor-at-Large for Fellowship Bible Church in Little Rock, Arkansas, where he served as Directional Leader for over 20 years. He is also Chairman of the Board of Fellowship Associates, a church consulting and leadership training organization, and Director of GlobalReach, a research and resource organization.

Robert is passionate about helping men discover the biblical principles of authentic manhood. He founded and developed *Men's Fraternity* in 1990. Today this significant area of ministry is reaching men worldwide in churches, on college campuses, in corporate boardrooms, and in prison cellblocks via his video curriculum, *Quest for Authentic Manhood, Winning at Work and Home,* and *The Great Adventure,* published by LifeWay. In response to great demand, Robert developed the feminine counterpart to *Men's Fraternity* in 2003, *The New Eve: 5 Guiding Lights to Authentic Womanhood in the 21st Century.*

He has authored a number of publications including *Raising a Modern-Day Knight* (Focus on the Family), the *Raising a Modern-Day Knight Video Training Series* with Dennis Rainey (Sonlight Productions), *Rocking the Roles: Building a Win-Win Marriage* (NavPress), *Real Family Values* (Multnomah Press) and *The Church of Irresistible Influence* (Zondervan). Robert's most recent book is *Culture Shift: Transforming Your Church From the Inside Out* published by Jossey-Bass. He is a contributing author to *Building Strong Families* edited by Dennis Rainey and *Faith Factor in Fatherhood* edited by Don Eberly. Robert has been featured on the radio programs FamilyLife Today and Focus on the Family, and in a number of magazines including *Leadership, Real Man,* and *Stand Firm.* Married since 1971, Robert and Sherard Lewis reside in Little Rock and have four children.

WELCOME TO THE GREAT ADVENTURE

Welcome to the Great Adventure! If you're like most men, it's easy in the frenzy of constant pressure and relentless responsibilities to lose your way. When we do, a life-numbing routine often replaces life-giving dreams. And when it does, the adventure and excitement of what my life means and where it's going becomes harder and harder to define.

Can life be an adventure again? Absolutely! And over the next 20 weeks, you will not only find out *how,* but ways that are within every man's reach. In fact, in these sessions we will have together, you will learn:

- How to live wisely with the end in mind
- How to develop a satisfying, personal mission for your life
- How to deal with unfinished business
- How to regain a sense of forward momentum for your life
- How to find your road to significance
- How to enlist teammates that get you there
- How to discover the best practices of successful men
- How to beat boredom and other opponents of Authentic Manhood
- How to focus your life
- How to leave a legacy in your life that blesses others
- And much more!

One of the special features of *The Great Adventure* is that you will have the opportunity to also discover *your unique design.* This dynamic personality inventory, along with several sessions of instructions, will enable you as a man to better understand who you are, how you're wired, and the unique way you enjoy and engage the world. Thousands of men have found this tool to be both eye-opening, difference-making, and life-changing. It allows you to see yourself, others, and your world as never before in a new and exciting way.

So are you ready for a change? Are you ready to pull your head up to catch a glimpse of just *how much more* there is out there for you?

If so, you're ready for the Great Adventure. Welcome aboard!

Robert Lewis

JOIN THE GREAT ADVENTURE

More than a rally or Bible study, Men's Fraternity provides men with an encouraging process that teaches them how to live lives of authentic manhood as modeled by Jesus Christ and directed by the Word of God. Men's Fraternity was developed by Robert Lewis over a number of years as he sought to connect with and challenge the men of his church. Now over 14 years later, over 1,400 men attend his weekly Men's Fraternity meetings at 6:00 in the morning. Men's Fraternity is being used by pastors and church leaders all over the world to energize the men of their churches and to connect with men in their communities.

Ways to Experience This Material

This life-changing curriculum is being experienced by thousands of men literally around the world in a variety of settings. Some of the most popular settings are:

A churchwide or even community-wide weekly setting where the lessons are presented on DVD or by a live presenter who has mastered the material. The large-group teaching time is followed by a small-group discussion where each man is able to process the truth he has heard with a group of his peers.

A small group of men who gather weekly at a church, office, or home to watch the DVDs or listen to the audio presentations and allow time for discussion.

A personal journey where some busy men choose to purchase the DVD or audio series to experience as they drive to work daily or travel on business.

Other settings include prisons, military bases, athletic teams, and college campuses.

This workbook is an essential tool for experiencing and processing Men's Fraternity, regardless in which setting you participate.

HOW TO GET THE MOST FROM MEN'S FRATERNITY

- Commit to attend all 20 sessions of *The Great Adventure*. These sessions build on one another, so don't miss any! Be a starter and a finisher. You'll be glad you did.
- Participate in the small-group discussion at the end of each session. Some of the questions you encounter each week may be hard to answer honestly, but your commitment to do so will help you and others. Believe that!
- Encourage the men in your small group. In any given week someone may be struggling and will need your help. Perhaps at some point you will need encouragement too.
- Take your assignments seriously. You will be asked to complete a personalized "Life Compass" by the end of the study. In addition, you will be asked to complete the online personality inventory "Servants by Design" after session 12. This inventory, which you will find at *www.youruniquedesign.com,* will be the focus of sessions 12–18. The cost of the inventory is $35. These application projects will make the information you receive each week come alive in your life! They will add valuable insight, understanding, and support to help you discover your own great adventure.
- Pray, asking God to use this series to help you become a better man. Ask Him in every session to speak to your heart, to open your eyes to wisdom, and to bless the interactions you will have with other men. Ask, and you will receive (see Matt. 7:7).
- If you have to miss a session of your Men's Fraternity study, you do not have to miss that session's presentation. Visit *www.mensfraternity.com* and click on "Missed a Session?" to listen to the session for a small fee.

For additional information, resources, and stories visit *www.mensfraternity.com* or *www.lifeway.com/mensfraternity.*

Session 1

STARTING THE GREAT ADVENTURE

I. Welcome to Men's Fraternity!

II. A Brief Men's Fraternity Orientation

III. The Goal of This Year's Men's Fraternity:

____

	MF1	MF2	MF3
NAME:			
FOCUS			
CHIEF ELEMENTS:			
MAJOR CHALLENGE:			
PASSION:			
DIRECTION:			

IV. Assumptions I Will Be Making

A. Our Creator desires for us to live a ________________ ________________.

B. Many men often miss this __________ _____ _________________ in their lives; others lose it somewhere along life's journey.

C. Men need ________________ ____________________ "to stay alive!"

D. An __________________________ man lives differently than others who blindly plod onward.

V. Promises for Any Man Who Completes All 20 Sessions

A. You will have opportunities to __________ _____________ about who you are and where you are going while making some significant, ________________ _________________________ in the process.

B. You will have the opportunity to __________________ with other men who can help you ________________ more clearly and objectively about your life.

C. You will learn how to ______________ your life using a __________ _____________ ________________________.

D. You will develop a personal ____________________ ______________________.

E. You will gain a better understanding of your _______________ ______________ and what makes you "___________ ____________".

F. You will have the opportunity to _____________ _____________ _____________!

1. Young men can get a ___________ _____________ on an exciting first half adventure in life.
2. Older men can _____________ for an exciting second half adventure in life.

QUESTIONS FOR YOUR SMALL GROUP

1. Make sure each man has had a chance to introduce himself. (Family, employment, why did you choose to enroll in Men's Fraternity, etc.?)

2. What stood out to you in this opening lecture of Men's Fraternity? Explain.

3. Which of the six promises made in session 1 was most appealing to you? Why?

Session 2

QUESTIONS EVERY ADVENTURER MUST FACE

I. Three Flashbacks from Last Week

A. Life for a man must be more than ____________________.

1. It can wear a man out.

2. It can pull a man down.

3. It can set a man up for a serious fall.

B. Life for a man needs to be woven with ________________________.

1. It means avoiding __________________ manhood.

2. It means finding a life balanced with …

- ____________________________
- ____________________________
- ____________________________
- ____________________________
- ____________________________
- ____________________________

C. This adventure we are exploring is ________ ______________ for most men.

1. We are in an age where "__________ __________"? is a growing question for men and __________ a growing need.

2. We are all __________ here.

II. Big, Hairy Questions

A. __________

B. __________

C. __________

Answer: __________/ __________ __________/ __________ __________

III. What Scripture Has to Say to BHQs.

A. I am a __________.

B. I am a __________.

	DEFINED AS:	WHO WITH:	KEY WORDS:	OUTCOME:
1. To __________ life	The __________ Adventure			
2. To __________ for a better life	The __________ Adventure			
3. To __________ life	__________ Adventures			

Key statement: __________

C. I am a man __________.

QUESTIONS FOR YOUR SMALL GROUP

1. What impacted you the most in today's message?

2. Which of the three adventures discussed in Session 2 is missing in your life? Why?

Session 3

PAUSING TO PROCESS

I. A Review of an Adventurer's BHQs

A. Three Questions

1. Who am I? ____.

2. Why am I here? ____.

3. Where am I going? ____.

B. Four Adventures (See chart on next page.)

II. 10 Practical Perspectives

A. These last two weeks have surfaced a lot of intense feelings in me. I'm not enjoying life as I should; I feel burdened by too much responsibility; I work too much; work consumes too much of me. Life is not an adventure.... Help!

B. You said last week, "Our work is to be a means to these three adventures (not an end to them)." ________ ____?

C. _____________ is Men's Fraternity going to help me find my adventure?

D. How do you make your family _____ __________________? Mine feels more and more like a grind. Where is the adventure in family?

E. How do I find those things that make me "__________ __________"?

F. I would like to have a ___________ to live for. How do I go about finding one?

Adventures	Defined	Teammates	Key Words	Outcome	Key Scripture
1. The Family Adventure ______ ______ ______	To Reproduce Life- ______ ______ ______	A Wife	• Understanding • Hands on involvement • Intimacy	• Legacy • Joy	Psalm 127:3-4 3 John 4 Proverbs 10:1
2. The Noble Cause Adventure ______ ______ ______	To Fight for a Better Life- ______ ______ ______	Like-Minded Partners	• Calling • Fit • Design • Contribution to the World	• Energy • Deep Satisfaction	Eph. 2:10 Titus 3:8 Acts 20:35 Eccl. 3:12 1 Tim. 6:18-19
3. Man-Size Adventures ______ ______ ______	To Enjoy Life- ______ ______	Friends, Especially Men Friends ______	• Explore • Challenge • Thrills	• Fun • Great Memories	Eccl. 3:22 Eccl. 5:18 Eccl. 9:9 1 Tim. 6:17
4. ______ ______ ______	______ ______ ______		• ______ • ______ • ______ • ______	• ______ • ______	1 John 5:11-13 John 10:10

G. How can I find some "______________" ______________________ to put the fun back into my life?

H. I'm in a job; I'm doing good; I'm making good money, but I just don't like what I do. I'm going through the motions and I hate that. ____________________________________?

I. I'm a young man just getting started. Life seems exciting enough to me now. How can I ____?

J. How ________________ are we going to be in here?

QUESTIONS FOR YOUR SMALL GROUP

1. What question asked today could you most identify with? Why? Was the answer a helpful start? What else do you need?

2. In light of these first three Men's Fraternity sessions, if you could wish for one thing right now, what would it be? Why?

3. Remember: This great adventure we are on is a process for every man. Solid answers that can help you capture the best in life take time, information gathering, and reflection. Let these sessions be that for you.

Session 4

THE ADVENTURER'S WIRING

I.

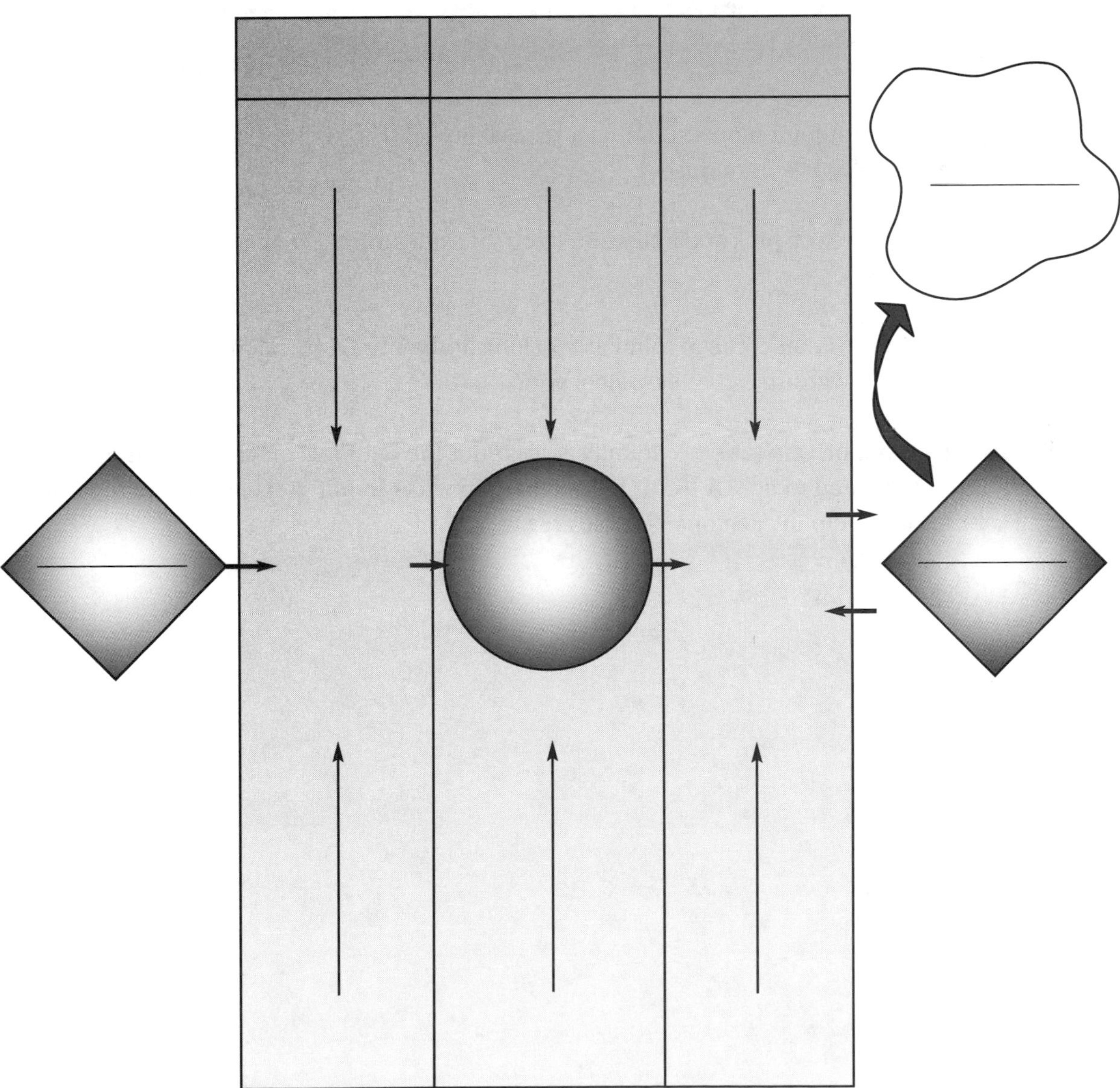

*Diagram adapted with permission from Bobb Biehl, *Focusing Your Life* (Quick Wisdom Publishing, 2001). As an executive coach, Bobb has many other helpful resources for men that can be found at *www.quickwisdom.com* or by calling (800) 443-1976.

II. Four Summary Observations

A. Knowing _______ _______________ is critical for understanding and rightly positioning my life.

B. The ________ is always with us for good or bad.

C. How we "__________" and "__________" the future affects our lives much more than most of us know.

D. The wise adventurer always lives with _______ ________ _____ _____________.

QUESTIONS FOR YOUR SMALL GROUP

1. Look over this diagram for a moment. Using it to test each of the "circuits" of your life, where would the obvious pluses and minuses be?

2. Share with your group one plus and one minus from your diagram. Explain why you picked those.

3. What are the questions that come to mind as you look at the minus you shared with your group? Is there any advice the group can offer to help you?

4. This week take some private time to carefully assess your life with this diagram. Are there some obvious things you need to do? Or learn? Or ask for help with? In our great adventure together, we will seek to offer help in each one of these areas.

Session 5

THE ADVENTURER'S SACRED OATH

I. Sacred Ground

A.

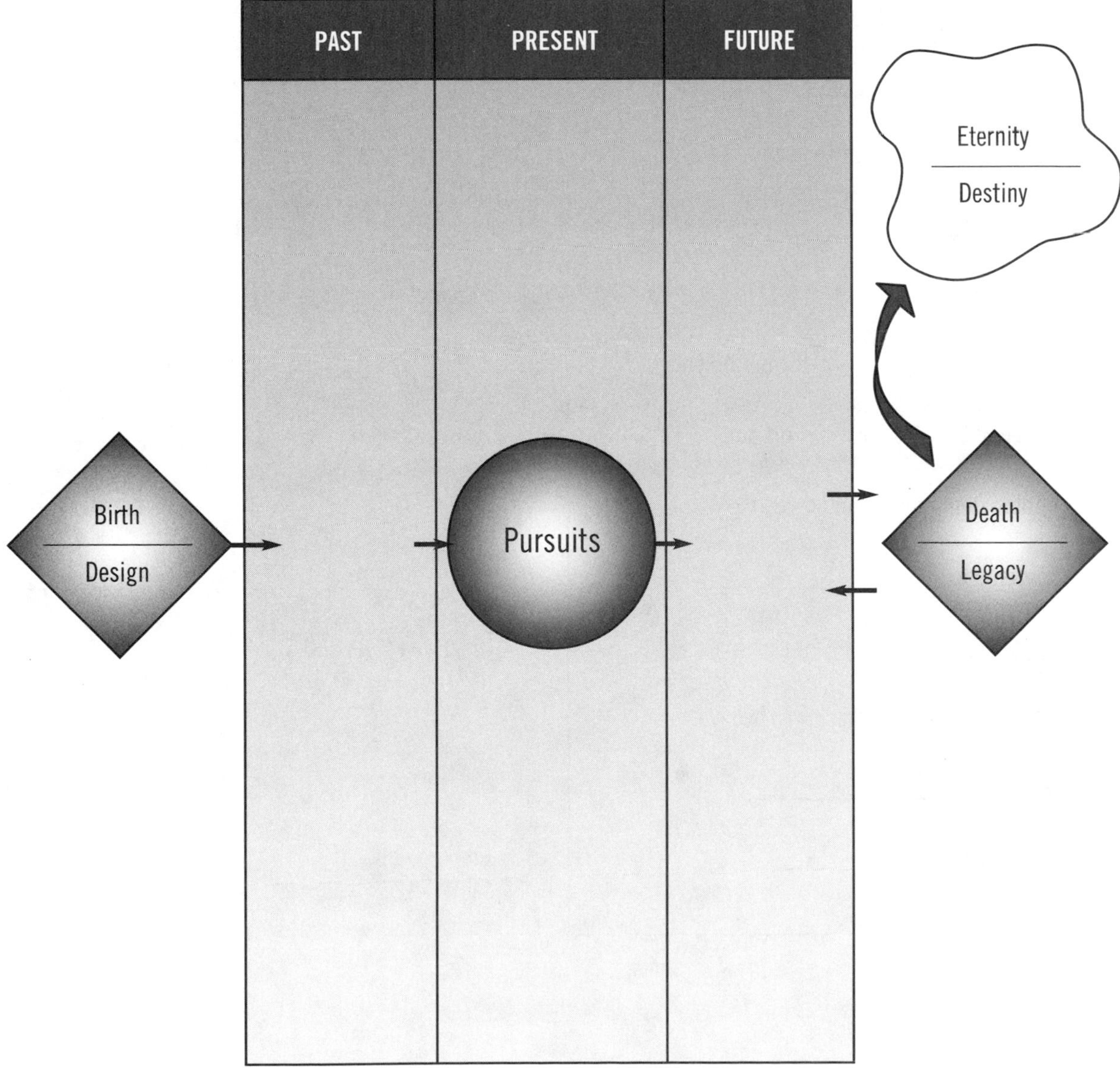

*Diagram adapted with permission from Bobb Biehl, *Focusing Your Life* (Quick Wisdom Publishing, 2001). See *www.quickwisdom.com.*

B. The Adventurer's Sacred Oath: ______________________________

______________________________.

II. Let's Get Metaphysical!

A. Metaphysics = ______________________________

B. Our World's Two Metaphysical Views of Life and Death

The Traditional/Religious Worldview	The Secular/Scientism Worldview
1. Says human beings are ______________ derived from __________	1. Says human beings are ______________ who have been derived from __________
2. Assumes what we can see and measure is ________________ to what we cannot see	2. Assumes what we can see and measure is ______________ — if not ______________ to any other reality
3. ____________ ______ the fulfillment of one of the strongest desires and anticipation of the human heart	3. _____________ the fulfillment of our heart's eternal longing
4. Points to a ______________________ ____________________ to our lives after death (and to those who believe, a happy ________________)	4. Points to a _______________ ______________ to our lives at death
5. Embraced by ____________________	5. Embraced by ______________________

C. Four Choices

1. ______________________________

2. ______________________________

3. ______________________________

4. ______________________________

III. Some Final Thoughts

A. An Adventurer always lives with ______________________.

Only with a clear and decisive view of ______________ can we ...

1. ______________________

2. ______________________

3. ______________________

B. Man has ________ ________ ________ when his belief goes no further than his life.

C. Avoiding conclusions about _____ ________ is essentially a vote for a ________ ________

__________ that eventually dead ends in frustration, unnecessary regrets, and fear.

D. If there is more to this life ________ __________, we should do all we can to understand

__________ __________!

QUESTIONS FOR YOUR SMALL GROUP

1. Practically, how would you like to finish this life? Share two dreams you have for your life. How are you living your life right now in light of those dreams?

2. What is one thing you personally believe about the end of life? Why do you believe that?

Session 6

TAKING THE GREAT ADVENTURE OUT OF THIS WORLD

I. Four Reflections from Last Week

A. Cultivating the "__________ ____________ __ _____ ______" is one of the most important things a man can do. With it, a man can "see" his life _____ _______ _______ which will be of great benefit to him now.

1. Sacred ground _________ _________ from this life's end.

2. Sacred ground _________ ____________ from this life's end.

B. The stronger the connection and fit between …

_____ __________ → ____ ___________ ____________ → ____ _______, the more meaningful and satisfying a man's life will be.

The Adventurer's Sacred Oath :____________________________

____.

C. LIFE as we know it turns on _________ ______________ ____________:

1. __________ _________! … after this life.

2. __________ _____________ _________!

D. DEATH as we know it offers us ___________ possible outcomes:

1. ____.

2. ____.

3. ____.

4. ____.

II. What's Next? A Christian Perspective

A. The Bible says ____.

So why has heaven lost weight with most men?

1. The only heaven most men know is ___________________________________.

2. We become consumed with trying _____________________________________.

3. We have rarely been offered a _______________________________________

____.

B. The Bible says heaven is a place of ...

1. ____

2. ____

- ____
- ____
- ____

3. ____

4. ____

5. ____

6. ____

C. The Bible says ________ ____________________ will go to heaven.

QUESTIONS FOR YOUR SMALL GROUP

1. What was the most meaningful thing you took from today's message? Explain your answer.

2. What did you learn about heaven that you didn't know before? Explain your answer.

3. If you had to give your final answer today, which one of the four possible outcomes at death would you choose as true? Explain your answer.

For knowing more about the subject of heaven and eternity, I would suggest you read *In Light of Eternity* by Randy Alcorn. It has short, concise, but meaty chapters—the kind of book men love!

Session 7

EVERY MAN'S ADVENTURE WITH ETERNITY

I. Some Opening Considerations

A. ___________ ___________________ are the most important decisions any man will make. Today, I will manage the affairs of my life, one way or the other, believing that ______ ________________ ...

- ____ (______________________________)
- ____ (______________________________)
- ____ (______________________________)
- ____ (______________________________)

B. What we believe about our finish and the future is called the _____________ _______________ ____ ________ _________. The more cultivated this _____________ is, the more fruitful will be my life now.

C. Every man believes "something" about _________ ________________ whether he admits it or not. You can't ___________ _________ ________ when it comes to eternal matters.

- To say ______ _______ ______ therefore __________________________ ... is actually a faith decision to reject all the religions of the world (option 3 and 4) and trust in either options 1 or 2.
- Tom Skinner : "I spent a long time trying to come to grips with _____ _______ and suddenly realized that I had better come to grips with ______ ___ ___________. I have since moved from the agony of questions that I cannot answer to the reality of answers I cannot escape ... and it's a great relief."

D. We ended last week with two questions concerning a purposeful universe (options 3 and 4) whose most meaningful endpoint was heaven.

1. ____?

2. ____?

II. What the Religions of the World Say

My Faith is in being ____________________	***My faith is in the help of a*** ____________________
Modern Judaism	Christianity
Islam	
Hinduism	
Buddhism	
Mormonism	

III. My Journey

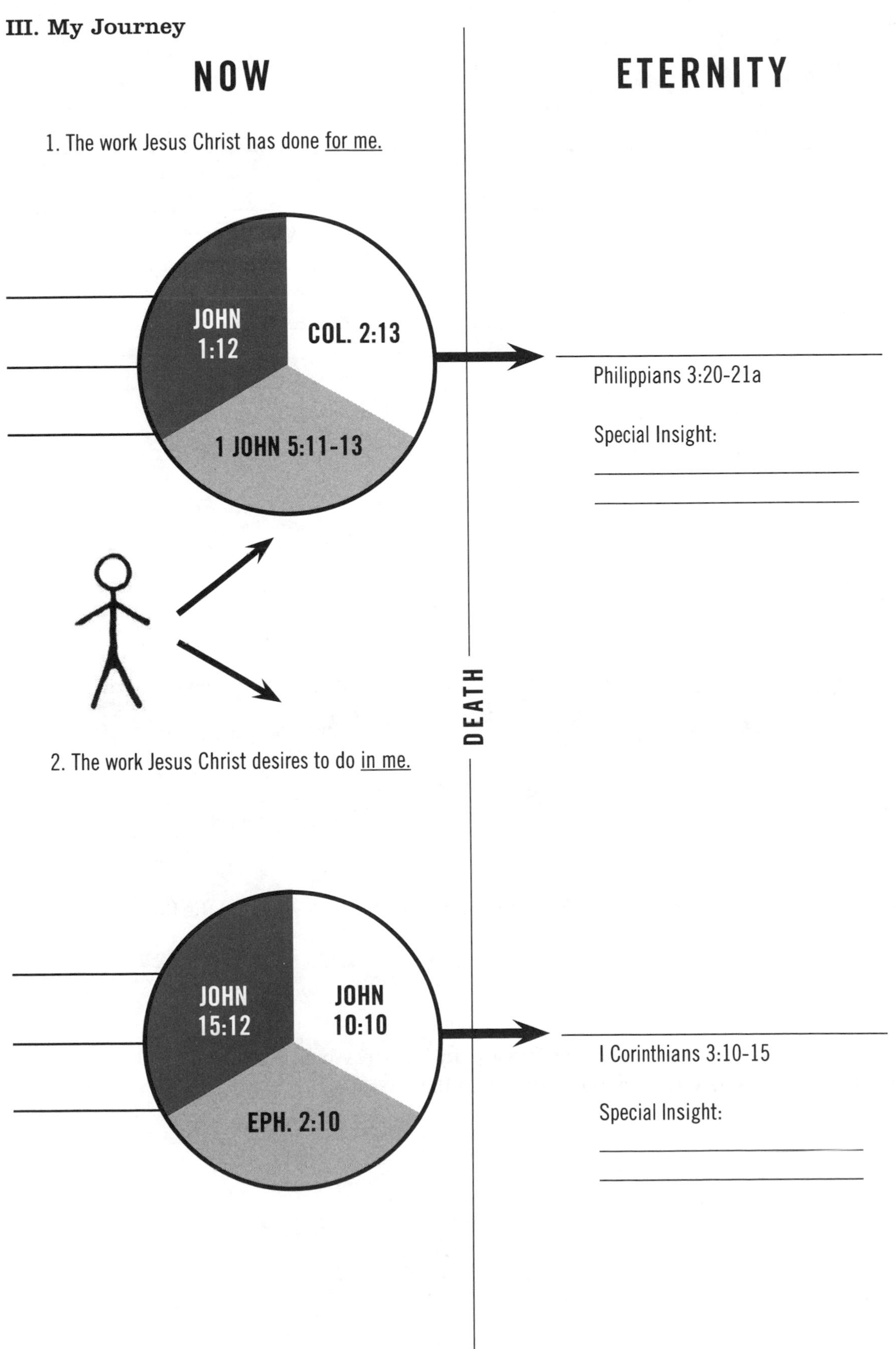

IV. Decision Time

A. So what do you believe?

1. ______________________________

2. ______________________________

3. ______________________________

4. ______________________________

B. Need help?

QUESTIONS FOR YOUR SMALL GROUP

1. What was the most important thing you heard today? Why?

2. At this point in your life, what have you concluded about eternity? What are the lingering questions you still have? How do you intend to find answers?

3. Do you need to investigate the claims of Christianity further? Would you be willing to talk to one of the leaders here today about how to start that investigation?

Session 8

REFOCUSING MY LIFE FOR ADVENTURE

I. Reviewing Our Wiring

A.

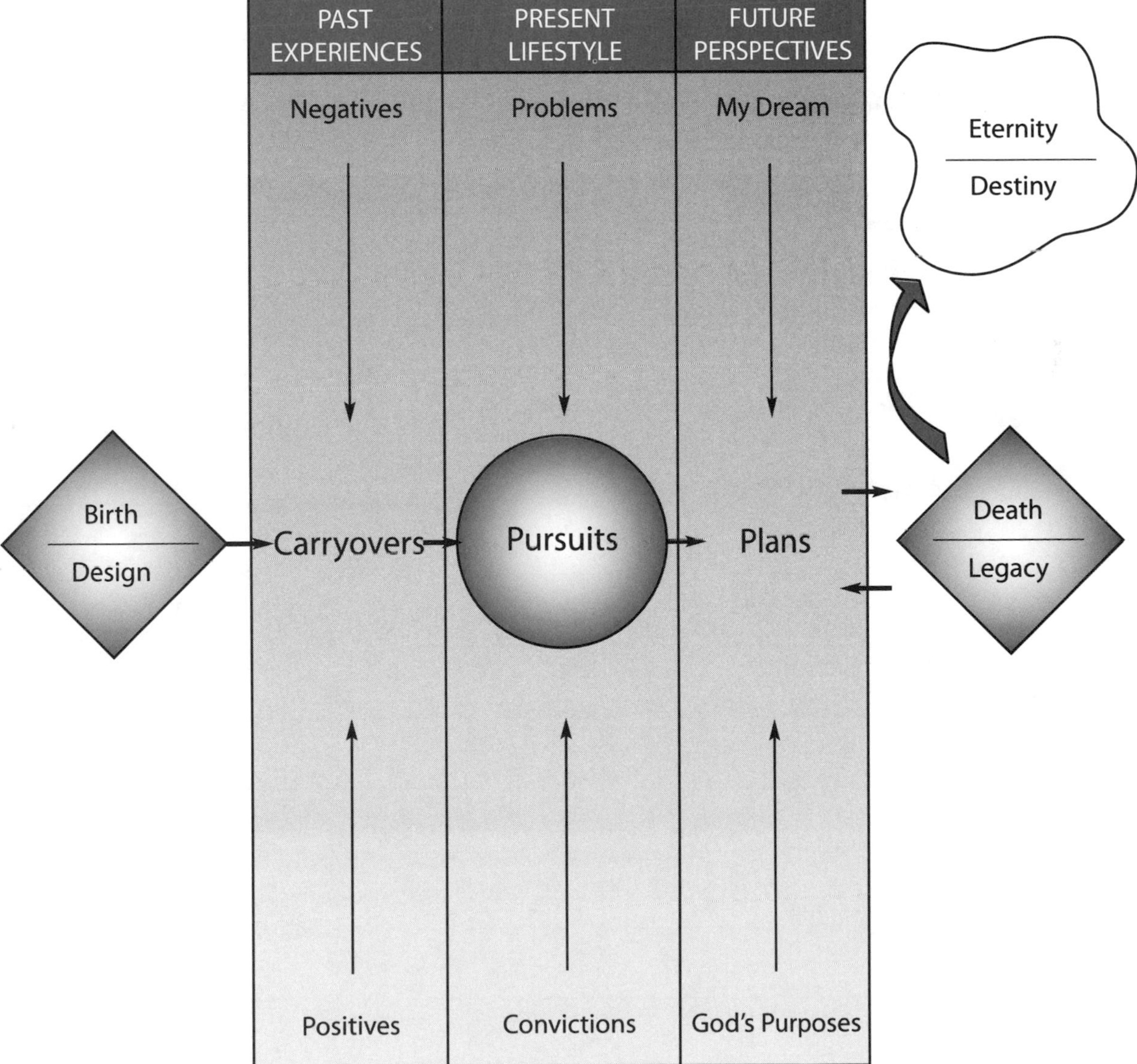

*Diagram adapted with permission from Bobb Biehl, *Focusing Your Life* (Quick Wisdom Publishing, 2001). See *www.quickwisdom.com.*

B. What We Have Learned So Far:

1. The real adventure turns on how well you're ____________________.

2. There are two ways to go through life:

- ____________/____________= __________ _____/ __________ _________
- ____________/____________= __________ _____/ __________ _________
- It's best to begin ________ _____ ________ ____ __________.

C. What We Have Covered So Far:

II. The Most Important Practical Project an Adventurer Can Ever Work On

A. Your North Star

Before I die, _____ __________ _________ . . .

_________ __________ __________ __________ __________ __________

B. Observations:

1. This is your opportunity to _____________ __________ ________ _________

rather than _______________ ____________ _______, even as a "success."

2. Be ________________ but not ________________ about your dreams.

3. Find ______________ to help you ____________________________.

4. It's never ________ __________ to start ________ _______________.

5. Young men will need to dream _______-__________ __________ _____________.

6. The younger you start this _______________ ______________, the greater __________

______________________(_______________________________)

____.

7. We will all start today with _____ _____________ and finish Men's Fraternity with a _____________ _____________.

QUESTIONS FOR YOUR SMALL GROUP

1. Share from your Sacred Ground Draft one or two dreams you feel are North Stars for you.

2. How would these fulfilled dreams make your life a more satisfying adventure? Explain.

**Remember! Today's draft is only a beginning.
You will need to keep pondering and polishing this project.**

— FIRST DRAFT —

SACRED GROUND

BEFORE I DIE, I WANT TO ...

	BE	DO	HAVE
1			
2			
3			
4			
5			
6			
7			
8			
9			
10			

Keeping my present pursuits in focus

HELP	ENJOY	LEAVE

*Diagram adapted with permission from Bobb Biehl, *Focusing Your Life* (Quick Wisdom Publishing, 2001). See *www.quickwisdom.com.*

Session 9

BEING ADVISED OF ADVENTURE BUSTERS, PART 1

I. A Vision to Live

II. Two Obstacles in Every Man's Adventure: A General Overview

A. The adventure through the lens of Hebrews 12:1

1. ____________________

2. ____________________

B. Four results of being __________ __________ and __________ _____.

1. __________

2. __________

3. __________

4. __________

III. Exploring the First Two Adventure Busters: A Specific Look

A. _____ __________ _______

1. Diagrammed:

Stated values __________ ________ actual behavior.

Stated values ________ ________ ________ ______ actual behavior.

Stated values _____________ __________ actual behavior.

Dysfunctional ←——————————→ **Functional**

- ____________________________________
- ____________________________________
- ____________________________________
- ____________________________________
- ____________________________________
- ____________________________________
- ____________________________________
- ____________________________________

2. Summarized:

- The greater the separation between our ____________ ________ and our _____________ ______________, the smaller our capacity for real ______________________.
- _______________ people often set themselves up for the ____________ ________.
- ____.

3. Safeguards:

- ______________________________/_________________________________
- ____

B. ______________ ____________________

1. ________ is (and should be) a wonderful part of the great adventure.

- ____________ is God's gift to us.
- ___________ ________ is the union of souls as well as _____________.
- ___________ ________ has ____________________________________.

2. ________ can also be a stumbling block to the great adventure.

3. Why men falter ...

- ____________________
- ____________________
- ____________________
- ____________________

4. Safeguards:

- For young men ... ____________
- ____________________
- ____________________

QUESTIONS FOR YOUR SMALL GROUP

1. What was the most important thing you heard from today's session? Why?

2. When it comes to sexual entanglements, where is your greatest vulnerability? Foolish fantasy? The need for emotional reassurance? Boredom? Arrogance? Explain.

Session 10

BEING ADVISED OF ADVENTURE BUSTERS, PART 2

I. A Brief Review

II. Life-Draining ________________ ______________

A. There is a Wrong Way to address these issues:

1. ________________ and seeking to solve the problem ____________.

2. Using ______________ to _________ my wife to adjust to my expectations.

3. The result: Growing __________________ _______ ____________ that, in time,

__________ ______ _______ _____________ and a major part of the adventure.

B. There is a Right Way to address these issues:

1. Keep ________________ and ________________.

2. Work to _____________________ even if I don't ______________.

Ask ________? and ____________! ____________ down her answers to be clear.

3. Be willing to say "_________________" for my _______________, regardless of how she responds.

4. Seek outside __________, sooner rather than later, when we can't find a satisfying __________.

5. Keep your ____.

III. Life-Defining ______________________

A. PTSD

B. A ________ defined: An unresolved ________ ______ ____

________ whose lack of ___________ adversely affects the quality

of a ______ _______ _____.

C. Some major ones in men's lives:

1. ______________________________

2. ______________________________

3. ______________________________

- ____________________________
- ____________________________
- ____________________________
- ____________________________
- ____________________________
- ____________________________

D. What we can do:

1. ______________________________

2. Seek ________ and get a plan for ______________.

3. Courageously address our __________ __________.

IV. Life-Paralyzing ______________________________

A. Do you know that you know that you know?

B. Major ___________ that swallow up the _____________:

1. ____________________

2. ____________________

3. ____________________

4. ____________________

5. ____________________

C. What we can do:

1. ________ ____________________

- Are others saying ... I have a ________________?
- If they are ... _____ ______! — regardless of how I feel.

2. ________ ____________________

- You ____________ beat an ________________ _____ ______________.
- You will need a _________ _______ _________ (God, counseling, family support, a sponsor and support program—AA, Celebrate Recovery, etc.).

V. A Final Word

- Everyone who "_________ _____ _____________" becomes a __________ and a ______________________ to others.
- Part of God's _____________ _________________ for any man is turning _________________ ________ __________________.

QUESTIONS FOR YOUR SMALL GROUP

1. What was the most important thing you heard in today's session? Explain.
2. What are the main adventure busters in your life? Explain.
3. What questions do you still have that need to be answered?

Session 11

ONE OF HISTORY'S BEST GREAT ADVENTURERS

I. A Brief Review

II. Observations on the Game of Life

A. How life generally shakes out:

1. ____________ .... ____________________________

2. ____________ .... ____________________________

3. ____________ .... ____________________________

4. ____________ .... ____________________________

B. Some helpful first and second ____________________________

____________________ ____________________

- Gary Chapman, *The Five Love Languages*
- Willard Harley, *His Needs, Her Needs*
- Robert Lewis, *Rocking the Roles: Building a Win-Win Marriage*
- Stu Weber, *Locking Arms*
- Patrick Morley, *Man in the Mirror*
- Bob Buford, *Halftime*
- Bobb Biehl, *Weathering the Midlife Storm*
- Patrick Morley, *Second Wind for the Second Half*
- Bob Buford, *Game Plan*
- John Eldredge, *Wild at Heart*
- Bobb Biehl, *Focusing Your Life*

C. Observations on how men play the game

1. Many men are stronger ________________________ than they are in the other.

- ________________________
    - ________________ - ________________
- ________________________
    - ________________ - ________________

2. Some men, on the other hand, live a ________________________

________________ ________________.

III. The Life of ________________

A. His Two Halves

1. The First Half: Numbers 13:1–14:32

- Key ingredient for success: ________________________
- Hard truth: ________________________
- Caleb's exhortation for today's young man: ________________________

2. The Second Half: Joshua 14:6-15

- Key ingredient for success: ________________________
- Hard truth: ________________________
- Caleb's exhortation for today's older man: ________________________

B. The Best of What This Great Adventurer Teaches Us

1. ________________ is never the deciding factor in life ...________________ is!

2. A real adventurer lives by an ________________ ________________ ... not by

________________ ________________ or ________________

________________ — and is richly ________________ for it.

3. Many of a man's greatest ____________________ are ________________ in the making:

    - ________________________
    - ________________________
    - ________________________
    - ________________________

4. Great adventurers empower the __________ ________________________ to reach ______________ and _____ __________ ________________.

IV. Practical "Take Homes" for Two Halves of the Great Adventure

A. For you young men:

1. Invest regularly in your ____________________ and make your __________ ________ ________ ____________.

2. Learn who you __________ and who you're _____________!

3. Always live within your _______________, stay out of ________________, learn to ______________ and ________ ________________.

4. Go for great __________________ over acquiring _________ _____________.

5. Get to know __________ _________________________.

6. Never stop fighting for _______________ and a ________ ____ _______________. It's the foundation for a successful second half.

7. Learn to ask for _____________________ ... from God and others.

8. Develop _______ ________________ you can love and be accountable to — _____ _____________ _____________.

9. Start developing and refining a ________________ ____________ a North Star for your life.

____

B. For you older men:

1. Don't ____________ ... ______________!

2. Make sure you know ________ ________ ________ ________ ________!

3. Build on your ___ ______________.

4. Clean up ______________ ______________:

______________, ______________, ______________,

make necessary ______________________.

5. Discover your ________ ________ and ________ others.

6. Invest in ____________ ________ ... whether you did it right or not.

7. Get to ________ ________ if you ________ ________ ________ of the first half ...

There's still time to do so!

8. Decide "________ ________" in the second half and then do it! Yearly, plan two or three

memory-making ___ __________________ for you and your wife.

9. Keep refining a ______________ ____________ for your life.

____

V. Conclusion

QUESTIONS FOR YOUR SMALL GROUP

1. What was the most important thing you heard in the session today? Why?

2. Looking back over this first semester, what has been the most significant thing you have learned and profited by? Why?

Session 12

YOUR UNIQUE DESIGN™

I. Promises ... Promises: A Quick Review of the First Semester

✓• You will have opportunities to think deeply about who you are and where you are going.

✓• You will have the opportunity to interact with other men who can help you think more clearly and objectively about your life.

✓• You will learn to focus your life using a Life Focus Chart.

✓• You will have the opportunity to choose your future.

- You will gain a better understanding of your ________________ ________________ and what makes you ____________ ____________.
- You will have the opportunity to develop a ________________ ______________ ________________________.

II. The Core Concept of Servants by Design™

"Most Americans do not know what their strengths are. When you ask them, they look at you with a blank stare or they respond in terms of subject knowledge, which is the wrong answer." —Peter Drucker

"Every person has been ____________ ____________ and ____________ by God to perform ________________ ____________ of service to ______ and ______ ____________."

III. Some Practical Benefits for You

A. Gain a ________________ ________________________ for your special ____________________

________ and ____________________.

B. Learn to ______________________ vocational and service opportunities with much greater

___________________ and ____________________.

C. Discover _________________ _____________ for connecting better _______________________

with all kinds of people.

D. Experience a _______ _________________ to _____________ your unique design in more

_________________ _________ to you and others.

QUESTIONS FOR YOUR SMALL GROUP

1. Can you fill in the blank? "When I ____________________, I feel God's pleasure." What are the times where you feel yourself "come alive"? Describe a couple of activities that really energize you. Share your answers with your group.

2. What are the implications of the Core Concept to you personally? Explain your answer.

3. Which of the four Practical Benefits is most important to you right now? Why?

VERY IMPORTANT! PLEASE READ!

To continue *The Great Adventure*™, every man must purchase and take the *Servants by Design*™ inventory online. It is also highly recommended that you purchase a *Servants by Design*™ *Profile Companion* to help you interpret your inventory.

Go to *www.youruniquedesign.com* and follow the instructions carefully. The inventory will take approximately 2 hours to complete.

When finished, your results will be e-mailed to you.

Instructions on how to fully understand these results will be given in sessions 13–18.

If you need computer assistance, please ask your leader for help.

Again, remember:

every man must take the Servants by Design™ inventory <u>before</u> session 14.

Bring your design results to sessions 14–18!

A Special Note to the Leader of Men's Fraternity

- Thoroughly review the frequently asked questions concerning the personality inventory that is found in your Leader Guide, as well as the Profile Companion you purchased online, before session 14.
- Be available to help your men better understand their inventories in whatever ways you can between sessions 14 and 18.

Session 13

EVIDENCE OF OUR UNIQUE DESIGN, PART 1

I. Review

A. You will gain a better understanding of your __________ __________ and what makes you

__________ __________.

B. You will have the opportunity to develop a __________ __________

__________.

THE CORE CONCEPT OF YOUR UNIQUE DESIGN

C. "Every person has been __________ __________ and __________ by God to perform

__________ __________ of service to __________ and to __________."

II. The Practical Benefits to You

A. A deeper appreciation for how God has __________ __________.

B. A greater clarity and confidence in evaluating new __________.

C. The discovery or invaluable insights for __________ __________with all kinds of people.

D. The experience of a __________ __________ to employ who you are in more meaningful ways.

III. Practical Evidence of Our Core Concept

A. Our __________ __________ is distinct.

B. Our __________ differ.

C. Our ______________ _______ __________________________ are not the same.

D. Our __________________ _____ ___________________ vary greatly.

- Function follows ______________________!

IV. Biblical Evidence of Our Core Concept

A. Foundational Principle #1

All that we are and have that is worthwhile is ____ ___________ ___________ __________ _______.

B. Foundational Principle #2

Some grace gifts are crafted by God at ___________________________ while others are given at __ ______________________________.

At Conception: Natural Abilities

For you created _____________'s inmost being; you knit ___________ together in his mother's womb. ____________ praises you because ________________ is fearfully and wonderfully made; your works are wonderful, ________________ knows that full well. ___________'s frame was not hidden from you when he was made in the secret together in the depths of the earth, your eyes saw his unformed body. All the days ordained for ____________ were written in your book before one of them came to be. Psalm 139:13-16

QUESTIONS FOR YOUR SMALL GROUP

1. What was the most important thing you heard today? Why?

2. The School for Animals teaches us that "function follows form" (unique design). How have you seen this in your children? Your wife? Your peers at work or close friends?

3. Reread Psalm 139:13-16. How do you feel about the way God made you? Explain. What purpose can you detect in your design? Explain.

4. Be sure you have your personality inventory in hand before our next session. Don't forget to bring it.

Because *Servants by Design*™ is copyrighted material, the session outline for sessions 14, 15, 16, 17 are found in a separate *Servants by Design*™ *Lecture Supplement* on pages 48–67.

We gratefully acknowledge Transpersonal Technologies for granting permission to include this supplement in *The Great Adventure*™.

SERVANTS BY DESIGN™

LECTURE SUPPLEMENT

Your Unique Design™ Edition

By Dr. Robert S. Maris and Dr. Jerry S. Richardson

Session 14

EVIDENCE OF OUR UNIQUE DESIGN, PART 2

"Every person has been uniquely crafted and gifted by God to perform meaningful tasks of service to Him and to others." (Our Core Concept)

I. Review: Evidence in Support of Our Core Concept

A. Practical Evidence "________________ ______________ __________."

B. Biblical Evidence

1. All that we are that is worthwhile is a ___________ __________ from God.

2. Some grace gifts are crafted by God at ____________________ while others are given at ______________________.

II. Today's Focus: Grace Gifts at Conversion

A. A Couple of Working Definitions

1. Conversion = ____________ ________ ________ _________ __________ ______according to Jesus, ___________________.

2. Spiritual gift = ____ ____.

B. Three Summary Truths About Spiritual Gifts: 1 Corinthians 12:4-11 (NASB)

Now there are varieties of gifts, but the same Spirit. And there are varieties of ministries, and the same Lord. There are varieties of effects, but the same God who works all things in all persons. But to each one is given the manifestation of the Spirit for the common good. For to one is given the word of wisdom through the Spirit, and to another the word of knowledge according to the same Spirit; to another faith by the same Spirit, and to another gifts of healing by the one Spirit, and to another the effecting of miracles, and to another prophecy, and to another the distinguishing of spirits, to another various kinds of tongues, and to another the interpretation of tongues. But one and the same Spirit works all these things, distributing to each one individually just as He wills.

1. Spiritual gifts are ______________________________.

2. Spiritual gifts are ______________________________.

3. Spiritual gifts are ______________________________.

III. Biblical Evidence: Foundational Principle #3

Your grace gifts crafted by God at conception (natural abilities) and those received at conversion

(spiritual gifts) should not be viewed as ______________ ______________

but rather as ______________.

IV. Servants by Design™ Profile

A. A Unique Condominium of Design Information: An Opening, Broad Overview

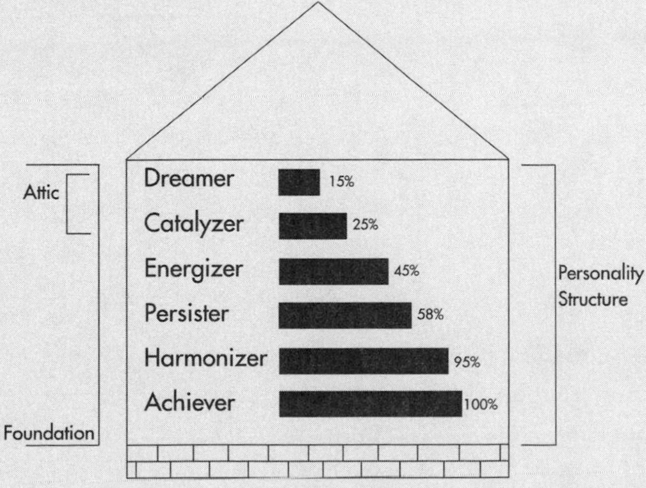

B. What's Next?

QUESTIONS FOR YOUR SMALL GROUP

1. What truth or principle presented has grabbed your attention the most in these sessions on design? Explain.

2. Using your *Servants by Design*™ Profile, identify the personality part you count on the most (nearest the foundation) ________________________ and the one you rely on the least (nearest the attic) ________________________. Share these with your group members as a start to processing your design information. Note how others in your group are like you or are different from you.

Special Note to the Leader of Men's Fraternity™

Before you break the men into their small groups, share with the men your answers to question 2. What does this say to you about yourself? How do you see this as true? Process your findings in front of the group before dismissing them to discuss their answers.

Session 15

UNDERSTANDING YOUR SERVANTS BY DESIGN™ PROFILE, PART 1

I. Review: Evidence of Unique Design

A. More Biblical Evidence At Conversion

B. Spiritual Gifts - A unique God-given ability that He uses to ____________ and ____________ His original design in your life.

1. Are ________________ ___________________ by the Holy Spirit

2. Are given for the ________________ ____ ____________

3. Are uniquely expressed with ___________ _____________

C. Foundational Principle #3

Your grace gifts crafted by God at conception (natural abilities) and those received at conversion (spiritual gifts) should not be viewed as _________________ but rather _________________.

II. Getting Acquainted with Your Personality Structure

A. Five Truths About Your Condominium

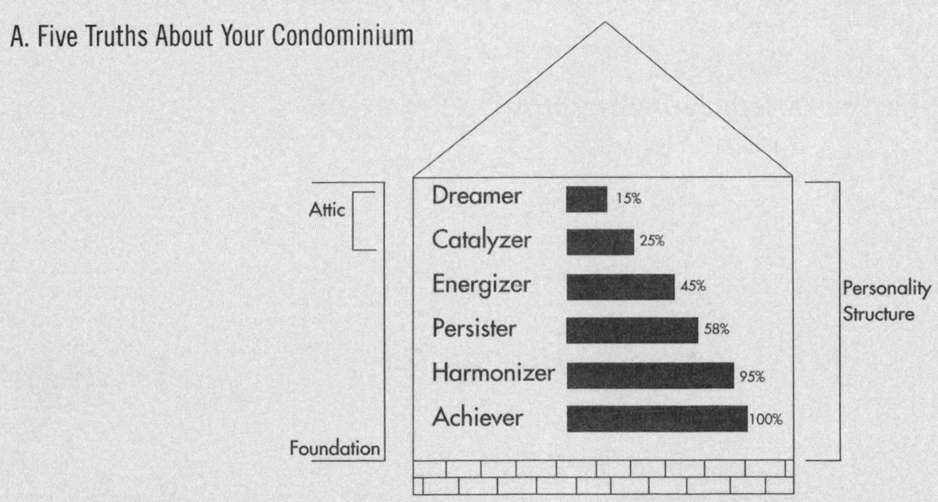

1. Your design is __________ __________________ to one __________________ __________

   but rather a ______________ ______________________ of all six.

2. Your _____ ______ represent the _________ _____ ___________ God has given you for each

   personality part.

3. Your ______________ ________________ are found in the personality parts closest to the

   ________________________.

4. Your personality parts nearest the _________ will be the ones you ___________ on least.

5. Understanding your unique _________________ ________________will help you discover

   your unique design from God.

B. Seven Specifics in Your Profile Report

- Strengths: The core assets of your unique design
- Viewpoint: The perspective from which you view life
- Motivators: The wants and needs that make you come alive
- Subject Matter: The resources you enjoy working with the most
- Abilities: The activities that describe how you go about doing things
- Setting: The environment in which you might best express your design
- Relationships: The type of supervision or leadership under which you will work most productively

III. Understanding the Strengths, Viewpoint, and Motivators of Each Personality Part

A. Harmonizer

- Strengths: ______________________, _______________, __________
- Viewpoint: _______________ first lens

- Motivator: needs recognition of ________________
- % of U.S. population: ____%; ____% are female, ____% are male
- Biblical example: Martha's sister Mary, Luke 10:38-42

B. Achiever

- Strengths: _____________, _______________, ____________________
- Viewpoint: _____________first lens
- Motivator: needs recognition of __________ and __________________________
- % of U.S. population: ____%; ____% are female, ____% are male
- Biblical example: Nehemiah, Nehemiah 2:6,11-18; 6:15-16

QUESTIONS FOR YOUR SMALL GROUP

1. What truth or principle presented today meant the most to you? Why?

2. Share with your small group one new insight you learned today about your unique condominium of design information. How is this beneficial to you?

Special Note to the Leader of Men's Fraternity™

Before the men break into their small groups, share with them the "seven specifics" in your profile report and what this confirms to you about your design. What new insights does it offer you? Explain.

Session 16

UNDERSTANDING YOUR SERVANTS BY DESIGN™ PROFILE, PART 2

I. Review: Getting Acquainted with Your Personality Structure

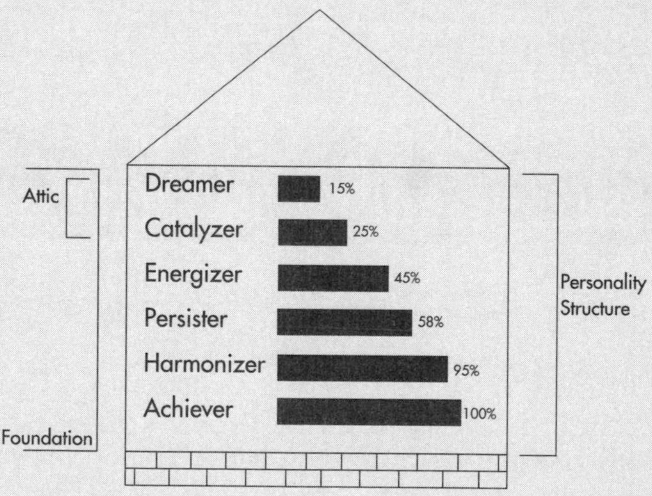

A. Five Truths About Your Condominium

- Your design is not limited to one personality part but rather a unique combination of all six.
- Your % bars represent the amount of energy God has given you for each personality part.
- Your greatest strengths are found in the personality parts closest to the foundation.
- Your personality parts nearest the attic will be the ones you rely on least.
- Understanding your unique personality structure will help you discover your unique design from God.

B. Reviewing the First Two Personality Parts

HARMONIZER

- Strengths: ________________________, ________________, __________
- Viewpoint: ________________ first lens
- Motivator: Needs recognition of _________________

ACHIEVER

- Strengths: ______________, ________________, _______________________
- Viewpoint: ______________first lens
- Motivator: Needs recognition of ______________ and ___________________________

II. Understanding the Strengths, Viewpoint, and Motivators of the Next Four Personality Parts

A. PERSISTER

- Strengths: _______________, ________________, _________________________
- Viewpoint: _________________________first lens
- Motivator: needs recognition of _______________________ and _________________
- % of U.S. population: ____%, ____% are female, ____% are male
- Biblical example: Paul, Philippians 3:4-9

B. DREAMER

- Strengths: ___________________, _________________________, _________________
- Viewpoint: ______________first lens
- Motivator: needs ________________ ____________ and ____________ _______________
- % of U.S. population: ____%, ____% are female, ____% are male
- Biblical example: Mary, the mother of Jesus, Luke 1:26-31; 2:16-19

C. CATALYZER

- Strengths: ______________________, ________________, ____________
- Viewpoint: _____________first lens
- Motivator: needs ___________ and opportunities to________________
- % of U.S. population: ____%, ____% are female, ____% are male
- Biblical example: Rahab, Joshua 2:1-16

D. ENERGIZER

- Strengths: ______________________, ______________________, __________
- Viewpoint: ___________________first lens
- Motivator: needs ________________ __________ and ________________
- % of U.S. population: ____%, ____% are female, ____% are male
- Biblical example: Peter, John 13:3-6, 8-9

QUESTIONS FOR YOUR SMALL GROUP

1. What insight did you gain today that helped you understand your unique design more completely? Share your insights with your group.

2. Look again at the various viewpoints of each personality part. How could understanding these enhance your communication with the others? Is there a friend, business associate, neighbor, or family member with whom you could make an immediate application? What is your application?

3. We will be addressing the writing of your Personal Mission Statement in detail next week. In the meantime, feel free to take a first pass at this during the week if you like, using the worksheet on the following pages.

DRAFT

WRITING YOUR PERSONAL MISSION STATEMENT

NAME: ____

Using your *Servants by Design*™ *Profile Report,* record your answers to the following statements. (A summary page of the strengths, viewpoints, and motivators of each personality part is attached to help you complete this project.)

Strengths (the core assets of **Servants by Design**™)

Your personality structure (condominium) indicates that your strongest personality parts are

(list 2 or 3): ____________ ________________ _________________

As a result, the descriptive words that best describe your strengths include: (use the attached summary page to guide your answers)

____

____

Viewpoint (the perspective from which you view life)

Because your base personality part (one nearest the Foundation) is __________,

you tend to view the world through a ________________ first lens.

Motivator (the wants and needs that make you come alive)

You are motivated by : ______________________________________

Subject Matter (the resources that you enjoy working with the most)

❒ data ❒ people ❒ things *(Check the one representing your highest score, as found in your Profile Report.)*

Record the activities under this area that you scored 70 percent or higher on.

____

____

Abilities (the activities that describe how you go about doing things)

Based upon the strengths of your personality, you have unique, God-given abilities in the following areas: (List up to five given in your Profile Report)

For each of these unique abilities, the descriptive statement that fits me best is:

____

____

____

Setting (the environment in which you might best express your design)

____

____

Relationship (the type of leadership or supervision under which you will work most productively)

____

____

Your Personal Mission Statement (According to ***Servants by Design***™)

With all of this information in mind, write a short mission statement in the box below that captures the essence of the real you. If possible, keep your description to 3-5 sentences.

2000 SAMPLE

God has designed me to use my organizational and relational abilities to lead, manage and encourage others. I feel His pleasure when He uses me to bring wisdom to a problem, accomplish a goal, develop a practical tool or conceptualize a clear process or system. God has designed me to communicate His truth to others with an emphasis on practical application.

YOUR FIRST PASS

God has uniquely designed me to ________________________________

____

____

____

Servants by Design™ Summary

SUMMARY PROFILE	CURRENCY	LANGUAGE
Harmonizer • Strengths: compassionate, sensitive, warm • Viewpoint: feeling first lens • Motivator: needs recognition of person	**Compassion**	Engage relationally with authentic caring
Achiever • Strengths: logical, organized, responsible • Viewpoint: thinking first lens • Motivator: needs recognition of ideas and accomplishments	**Logic**	Engage with accurate information and measurable results
Persister • Strengths: dedicated, observant, conscientious • Viewpoint: evaluating first lens • Motivator: needs recognition of beliefs and convictions	**Values**	Engage with assurance of commitment and loyalty
Dreamer • Strengths: imaginative, reflective, calm • Viewpoint: reflecting first lens • Motivator: needs private time and personal space	**Imagination**	Engage with clear direction and steps of action
Catalyzer • Strengths: adaptable, persuasive, charming • Viewpoint: acting first lens • Motivator: needs excitement and opportunities to make things happen	**Charm**	Engage with energy and a readiness to initiate
Energizer • Strengths: spontaneous, creative, playful • Viewpoint: reacting first lens • Motivator: needs playful contact and humor	**Playfulness**	Engage with upbeat comments and humor

Session 17

WRITING YOUR PERSONAL MISSION STATEMENT

I. Review: Character Descriptions

PERSONALITY PART	VIEWPOINT	CURRENCY
A. ____________	"I ________ "	____________
B. ____________	"I ________ "	____________
C. ____________	"I ________ "	____________
D. ____________	"I ________ "	____________
E. ____________	"I ________ "	____________
F. ____________	"I ________ "	____________

*Determine which ____________ a person is ________ ____ and speak his/her ____________ when you want to ________ .

II. Project: Writing Your Personal Mission Statement

NAME: ____

Using your *Servants by Design*™ *Profile Report,* record your answers to the following statements. (A summary page of the strengths, viewpoints, and motivators of each personality part is attached to help you complete this project.)

Strengths (the core assets of your unique design)

Your personality structure (condominium) indicates that your strongest personality parts are

(list two or three): ____________ ______________ ________________

As a result, the descriptive words that best describe your strengths include: (use the attached summary page to guide your answers) ____

____

____

Viewpoint (the perspective from which you view life)

Because your base personality part (one nearest the Foundation) is __________, you tend to view the world through a ________________ first lens.

Motivator (the wants and needs that make you come alive)

You are motivated by : ____________________________________

Subject Matter (the resources that you enjoy working with the most)

❒ data ❒ people ❒ things

(Check the one representing your highest score, as found in your Profile Report.)

Record the activities under this area that you scored 70 percent or higher on.

____

____

____

Abilities (the activities that describe how you go about doing things)

Based on the strengths of your personality, you have unique, God-given abilities in the following areas:

(List up to five given in your Profile Report)

For each of these unique abilities, the descriptive statement that fits me best is:

____

____

____

____

____

Setting (the environment in which you might best express your design)

____

____

____

Relationship (the type of leadership or supervision under which you will work most productively)

____

____

Your Personal Mission Statement (According to Servants by Design™)

With all of this information in mind, write a short mission statement in the box below that captures the essence of the real you. If possible, keep your description from three to five sentences.

2000 SAMPLE

God has designed me to use my organizational and relational abilities to lead, manage and encourage others. I feel his pleasure when He uses me to bring wisdom to a problem, accomplish a goal, develop a practical tool or conceptualize a clear process or system. God has designed me to communicate His truth to others with an emphasis on practical application.

2001 SAMPLE

God has uniquely designed me to use my unique organizational and relational abilities to accomplish a significant task or bring practical wisdom and encouragement to others. My primary focus is teaching and mentoring church leaders, men in transition, and members of Fellowship Bible Church.

QUESTIONS FOR YOUR SMALL GROUP

1. Take a moment and write out a first pass personal mission statement:

YOUR FIRST PASS

God has uniquely designed me to ____________________________________

2. Share your mission statement with the group and tell why.

Session 18

DESIGN ENCOURAGEMENTS

I. Review: From Information to Application

A. Speaking Another Person's Language

B. Writing Your Personal Mission Statement

SAMPLE

God has uniquely designed me to use my unique organizational and relational abilities to accomplish a significant task or bring practical wisdom and encouragement to others. My primary focus is teaching and mentoring church leaders, men in transition, and members of Fellowship Bible Church.

II. Seven Encouragements for Your Great Adventure Process

A. Reduce your ____________ _________________ to a ___________ to a __________.

B. Pursue the __________ that make you ____________ ______________.

C. Say ______ or _____ to opportunities based on your ___________ ___________ from __________.

D. Include your ___________ in your ____________ __________________ process.

E. Be _____________ about _______________ ___________ ___________.

F. Form a _____________ ___________ to ____________ for you and hold you

_________________________.

G. Keep your ____________ in focus by using your ________________.

QUESTIONS FOR YOUR SMALL GROUP

1. What was the most important thing you heard in today's session? How did it impact you? Explain.

2. Could you state your personal mission in a word? If so, what would it be? How did you arrive at this simple, descriptive word for the "real you"? Explain.

The Great Adventure Book List

A number of men have found one or more of the following resources helpful in stimulating their thinking about design wiring and what they have been created to do with their lives. I hope at least one of these will be beneficial to you.

- Donald Clifton and Paula Nelson, *Soar with Your Strengths* (Dell Publishing, 1995)
- Tom Paterson, *Living the Life You Were Meant To Live* (Nelson Books, 1998)
- Marcus Buckingham and Donald Clifton, *Now, Discover Your Strengths* (Free Press, 2001)

SACRED GROUND

BEFORE I DIE, I WANT TO ...

	BE	DO	HAVE
1			
2			
3			
4			
5			
6			
7			
8			
9			
10			

Keeping my present pursuits in focus in light of my design discoveries and personal mission statement

HELP	ENJOY	LEAVE

*Diagram adapted with permission from Bobb Biehl, *Focusing Your Life* (Quick Wisdom Publishing, 2001). See *www.quickwisdom.com.*

SESSION 19

HOW TO BE A GREAT ADVENTURER

I. It's Great to Be a Man!

II. Defining Moments

A. Every man has a few ________________ ____________________________ in his life where he goes to a place inside himself and decides …

1. Who he will ___________

2. What he will give his life to _________________________

3. How much effort he will give before he ________________

B. In the critical moments of life, real adventurers will step forward and choose

____

C. The Scripture acknowledges the importance of these defining moments:

1. Joshua 24
2. Deuteronomy 30

D. The key now to being a great adventurer ____________________!

- ___________ _____________ ________________________
- ___________ _____________ ________________________
- ___________ _____________ ________________________
- _______ ______ ______ _________ ____ ____ ___________

E. The final steps of authentic manhood and adventure you must take ________________. Don't expect

______________, your ___________ or another ______________ to carry you there!

III. How to Put Your Great Adventure Together and Make it Work!

A. You must set aside ____

1. About ________________________ _________________________________

2. Over ____

3. Filling out ____

*Be sure to ask God to join you and help you in this quiet time.

B. You would be wise to interact with two or three _________ _________________ about your thoughts

and conclusions (I would include my wife in this). Make appropriate refinements.

C. Decide on a ________________ __________________ of action.

1. Use your wiring to prioritize.

2. Use "Four Adventures of a Man" to prioritize.

3. Use "My Life Compass" to prioritize.

D. Take courage and start your great adventure by addressing ___________ _____________

________________________. Some examples …

- Job
- Marriage
- Wounds holding me back
- Fun
- Noble cause
- Spiritual life

IV. Looking for Calebs

QUESTIONS FOR YOUR SMALL GROUP

1. At this point in your great adventure, what is still missing? Explain.

2. What was said today that makes you swallow hard? Can you tell why?

3. What is the most important next step in your great adventure? Explain.

4. Have you completed a solid first pass on your Life Compass? Let your group know.

****

BE THINKING OF ONE MAJOR BENEFIT TO YOU
OF THIS YEAR'S MEN'S FRATERNITY.

WHAT IN YOUR LIFE HAS CHANGED OR IMPROVED
BY THE MATERIAL WE'VE COVERED?

BE PREPARED TO SHARE THIS AT GRADUATION NEXT WEEK!

DON'T MISS FINISHING!

Session 20

FINAL THOUGHTS

I. The Sword of Manhood

A. Real manhood is a ________________ … _______ ___________ ___________!

B. I Timothy 1:18

II. The Inward Thrust of the Sword

A. Against ____________________________

B. Against ____________________________

1. Do I have _____________ ___________ _____________________________?

2. What do _____ ____________ … __________ ______________________?

III. The Forward Thrust of the Sword

A. To conquer ______________________________ in my life

B. To acquire clear _________________________ for my life

C. To persevere and take ______________ _______________ with my life

IV. The Upward Thrust of the Sword

A. To celebrate ________________________

B. To celebrate a life ___________ _____________ with the expectation of ______ ______ ________

Answer Key

SESSION 1

II-Name/MF1:	The Quest for Authentic Manhood
II-Name/MF2:	A Man at Work and at Home
II-Name/MF3:	A Man and His World: The Great Adventure
II-Focus/MF1:	A Man's Core Identity
II-Focus/MF2:	A Man's Chief Responsibility
II-Focus/MF3:	A Man's Chosen Destiny
II-Chief/MF1:	A Man's Wounds; Definition of Manhood; Overview of Manhood Issues
II-Chief/MF2:	How a Man Enjoys His Work; How a Man Relates Successfully to a Woman
II-Chief/MF3:	Rediscovering the Adventure of Life; Understanding His Design; Developing a Satisfying Life Focus
II-Major/MF1:	The Boy in You Must Die
II-Major/MF2:	The Man in You Must Step Forward
II-Major/MF3:	The Adventurer in You Must Live
II-Passion/MF1:	Seizing Your Manhood
II-Passion/MF2:	Establishing Your Manhood
II-Passion/MF3:	Maximizing Your Manhood
II-Direction/MF1:	Go
II-Direction/MF2:	Fight
II-Direction/MF3:	Win
III: Goal	To help you finish this life with satisfaction and enter the next life with confidence
IV-A:	meaningful adventure
IV-B:	spirit of adventure
IV-C:	ongoing adventure
IV-D:	adventuresome
V-A:	think deeply/personal discoveries
V-B:	interact/think
V-C:	focus/Life Focus Chart
V-D:	mission statement
V-E:	unique design/come alive
V-F:	choose your future!
V-F1:	jump start
V-F2:	retool

SESSION 2

I-A:	responsibility
I-B:	adventure
I-B1:	half-life
I-B2:	A sense of purpose/Calling/ Fit/Fun/Energy/Destiny
I-C:	new territory
I-C1:	"what else"?/self-management
I-C2:	pioneers
II-A:	Who Am I?
II-B:	Why Am I Here?
II-C:	Where Am I Going?
Answer:	Guesswork/Cultural Conformity/Age-Old Wisdom
III-A:	man created by God
III-B:	man commissioned by God
III-B1:	reproduce
Defined As:	Family
Who With:	A Wife
Key Words:	Understanding Hands-On Involvement/Intimacy
Outcome:	Legacy/Joy
III-B2:	fight
Defined As:	Noble Cause
Who With:	Like-Minded Partners
Key Words:	Calling/Fit/Design / Contribution to the World
Outcome:	Energy/Deep Satisfaction
III-B3:	enjoy
Defined As:	Man-Sized

Who With:	Friends, especially men friends
Key Words:	Explore/Challenge/Thrills
Outcome:	Fun/Great Memories
Key Statement:	Your job should be a means to these three adventures (not an end to them.)
III-C:	who will ultimately face God.

SESSION 3

I-A1:	I am a man created by God.
I-A2:	I am a man commissioned by God.
I-A3:	I am a man who will ultimately face God.
I-B1-Adventures:	God said be fruitful and multiply
I-B1-Defined:	In my children
I-B2-Adventures:	Subdue the earth
I-B2-Defined:	Make this world better for others
I-B3-Adventures:	God blessed them
I-B3-Defined:	For myself
I-B4-Adventures:	Spiritual Life, God
I-B4-Defined:	To experience spiritual life and have more than this life alone offers.
I-B4-Teammates:	God
I-B4-Key Words:	Faith/Love/Worship/Follow
I-B4-Outcome:	Peace/Eternal Life
II-B:	Can you elaborate?
II-C:	When
II-D:	an adventure
II-E:	come alive
II-F:	cause
II-G:	man-size adventures
II-H:	What should I do
II-I:	avoid ending up where most of you old guys seem to be
II-J:	religious

SESSION 4

SEE DIAGRAM on page 15

II-A:	my design
II-B:	past
II-C:	see/embrace
II-D	the end in mind

SESSION 5

I-B:	I will fervently live my life according to my design, with the end in mind.
II-A:	Peripheral Vision
II-B1-left column:	the less/the more
II-B1-right column:	the more/the less
II-B2-left column:	secondary
II-B2-right column:	primary/exclusive
II-B3-left column:	Allows for
II-B3-right column:	Denies
II-B4-left column:	meaningful continuance/continuance
II-B4-right column:	meaningless ending
II-B5-left column:	faith
II-B5-right column:	faith
II-C1:	That's all, folks! ... The "Dead End" Option
II-C2:	It's not the end, but everything will be OK. ... The Blind Optimist Option
II-C3:	It's not the end, but I'll be OK. ... The "I'm Good Enough" Option
II-C4:	It's not the end, but I'm uncertain and uneasy. ... The "I Need Help" Option
III-A:	the end in mind/the end
III-A1:	Pursue life with a balanced and healthy perspective
III-A2:	Leave behind a satisfying legacy
III-A3:	Be ready and confident about eternity
III-B:	never done well
III-C:	the end/"now only" lifestyle
III-D:	than death/what's next

SESSION 6

I-A:	sacred ground of the mind/ at the end
I-A1:	looks back
I-A2:	looks forward
I-B:	My design / My present pursuits/My end
I-B Oath:	I will fervently live my life according to my design with the end in mind.
I-C:	two worldviews
I-C1:	There's more
I-C2:	There's nothing more
I-D:	four
I-D1:	It's over
I-D2:	It's not over, and whatever's next, everyone will be fine.
I-D3:	It's not over, and I'm good enough for what's next.
I-D4:	It's not over, and I will need help for what's next.
II-A:	death offers the possibility of great gain
II-A1:	childish and boring
II-A2:	to build a heaven for ourselves here
II-A3:	biblical vision of heaven that's compelling and motivating
II-B1:	Resolution, namely to this life's loose ends
II-B2:	Altered states
II-B2a:	New bodies
II-B2b:	New relationships
II-B2c:	New home
II-B3:	Personal rewards
II-B4:	New status and positions for everyone
II-B5:	Action and new adventures
II-B6:	Endless surprises
II-C:	not everyone

SESSION 7

I-A:	Faith decisions/in eternity
I-A1:	Nobody sees and nobody cares/(Meaningless Universe)
I-A2:	Somebody sees but it doesn't matter./(Amoral Universe)
I-A3:	Somebody sees and is keeping score./(Purposeful Universe)
I-A4:	Somebody sees and wants to help./(Purposeful Universe)
I-B:	sacred ground of the mind/ ground
I-C:	his finish/take the fifth
I-C1:	you can't know/I will not believe in anything
I-C2:	my doubts/what I believe
I-D1:	How good do you have to be to merit heaven?
I-D2:	Is there another way besides having to be good enough?
II-left heading:	"good enough"
II-M. Judaism:	Anyone, Jew or not, may gain heaven through commitment to one God and moral living. Judaism believes in afterlife but does not stress preparing man for it.
II-Islam:	Man earns heaven by good works as declared in the Koran. Hell is for those who oppose Allah and his prophet Mohammed.
II-Hinduism:	Man earns heaven through devotion, meditation, good works and self-control. If he fails to succeed, he may try again in a reincarnated form.
II-Buddhism:	Man gains heaven by self effort only in following Buddha's eightfold path to enlightenment.
II-Mormonism:	All men will spend eternity on some level of a

	multistoried heaven. The level will be determined by the scope of each man's work.
II-right heading:	Savior
II-Christianity:	No one can earn heaven by getting better. Man obtains heaven, as well as the best of this life, with the help of Jesus Christ. Jesus boldly summed it up this way: "I am the way, the truth, and the life." John 14:6
III-1-John 1:12:	Makes me a child of God
III-1-Col. 2:13:	Forgives all my sins
III-1-I Jn. 5:11-13:	Gives me eternal life
III-1-3 left lines:	Can't Improve/Can't Fall Out/Permanent
III-1-Phil. 3:20-21a:	Guarantees heaven
III-1-Special Insight:	I am secure in Christ forever
III-2-Jn. 15:12:	Helps me love others
III-2-Jn. 10:10:	Helps me experience abundant life
III-2-Eph. 2:10:	Helps me do good works
III-2-3 left lines:	Can improve / Can Fall Out/Dynamic
III-2-I Cor. 3:10-15:	Earns or forfeits rewards
III-2-Special Insight:	I am responsible to Christ every day.
IV-A1:	It's over
IV-A2:	It's not over, and whatever is next, everyone will be fine.
IV-A3:	It's not over, and I'm good enough for what's next.
IV-A4:	It's not over, and I will need help for what's next.

SESSION 8

I-A:	SEE DIAGRAM on page 15
I-B1:	wired
I-B2a:	Comparing/Competing = The Reactive Life/Unhealthy Pressure
I-B2b:	Envisioning/Enjoying = The Proactive Life/Healthy Pursuits
I-B2c:	with the end in mind.
II-A:	I want to ... BE/DO/HAVE/HELP/ENJOY/LEAVE
II-B1:	proactively craft your adventure/wandering through life
II-B2:	realistic/restrictive
II-B3:	someone/dream
II-B4:	too late/the adventure
II-B5:	first-half dreams primarily
II-B6:	proactive process/the return of reward (rather than regret) adventure and, yes, nobility
II-B7:	a draft/solid plan

SESSION 9

II-A1:	Wrong headedness that slows us down
II-A2:	Wrongdoing that holds us back
II-B:	weighed down/tangled up
II-B1:	Less
II-B2:	Hard rebuilding
II-B3:	Bondage
II-B4:	Despair
III-A:	The Double Life
III-A1:	conflict with/ebb and flow with/consistently match
III-Dysfunctional:	Marriage is shallow Children are wounded Noble cause undermined Spiritual judgment
III-Functional:	Marriage is intimate (trust) Children are healthy Noble cause enhanced Spiritual blessing
III-A2a:	public face/private behavior/adventure
III-A2b:	Religious/double life
III-A2c:	Integrity is just healthy.
III-A3a:	Real conclusions/Written convictions

III-A3b:	Have friends you are accountable to!
III-B:	Sexual Shortcuts
III-B1:	Sex
III-B1a:	Sex
III-B1b:	Great sex/bodies
III-B1c:	Great sex/boundaries
III-B2:	Sex
III-B3a:	Foolish fantasy, ignorant of consequences
III-B3b:	The deep need in men for emotional reassurance
III-B3c:	Boredom
III-B3d:	Arrogance
III-B4:	Faith
III-B41:	Friends you're accountable to
III-B42:	Making time to love and enjoy your wife

SESSION 10

II:	Marriage Problems
II-A1:	Withdrawing/alone
II-A2:	intimidation/force
II-A3:	frustration and anger/ closes off the heart
II-B1:	learning/growing
II-B2:	understand/agree/ why/listen/ Write
II-B3:	I'm sorry/sorry behavior
II-B4:	Help/Resolve
II-B5:	conflict accounts short
III:	Wounds
III-B:	wound/issues from the past/ closure/man's life now
III-C1:	The Father Wound
III-C2:	The Overly Controlling Mother Wound
III-C3:	Trauma Wounds
III-C3 bullets:	Abuse/Rape/Divorce/ Suicide of a Parent/ Death of a Parent/ An awful church experience growing up
III-D1:	Identify the wound.
III-D2:	help/healing
III-D3:	wound head-on
IV:	Addictions
IV-B:	addictions/adventurer
IV-B1:	Sexual addiction
IV-B2:	Drug addiction
IV-B3:	Alcohol addiction
IV-B4:	Anger addiction
IV-B5:	Gambling addiction
IV-C1:	Get honest
IV-C1a:	problem
IV-C1b:	I do
IV-C2:	Get real
IV-C2a:	cannot/addiction by yourself
IV-C2b:	team to win
V-1:	beats a buster/hero/life-giver
V-2:	great adventure/negatives into positives

SESSION 11

II-A1:	1–20, Warm-ups
II-A2:	20–40, First half of play
II-A3:	40–50, Halftime adjustments
II-A4:	50–?, Second half of play
II-B:	half coaches/First-Half Coaches/Second-Half Coaches
II-C1:	in one half of the game
II-C1a:	Strong First Half/David/ Solomon
II-C1b:	Strong Second Half/Moses/ Matthew
II-C2:	complete, Great Adventure
III:	Caleb
III-A1a:	raw faith
III-A1b:	Many young men often wander around in life and squander their strengths.
III-A1c:	Take the land (the promised life)
III-A2a:	Fresh Faith
III-A2b:	Many older men often settle down in the lowlands and squander their assets.

III-A2c:	Take the high ground! (the best of life)
III-B1:	Background/faithground
III-B2:	inner vision/outward circumstances/cultural pressure/rewarded
III-B3:	victories/decades
III-B3 bullets:	Great Marriage/Noble Character/Healthy Productive Children/Greatest Accomplishments and Noble Cause
III-B4:	next generation/high/ do great things.
IV-A1:	marriage/wife your best friend
IV-A2:	are/not
IV-A3:	means/debt/save/give away
IV-A4:	experiences/more stuff
IV-A5:	God personally
IV-A6:	purity/life of integrity
IV-A7:	forgiveness
IV-A8:	men friends/a personal board
IV-A9:	long-range vision
End Statement:	Take this land with Raw Faith!
IV-B1:	retire ... refocus!
IV-B2:	what makes you come alive!
IV-B3:	strengths
IV-B4:	unfinished business: reconcile, forgive, apologize/ restitution
IV-B5:	noble cause/serve
IV-B6:	younger men
IV-B7:	know God/left Him out
IV-B8:	what's fun/experiences
IV-B9:	long-range vision
End Statement:	Take this High Ground with Fresh Faith!

SESSION 12

I-A:	unique design/come alive
I-B:	personal mission statement
II:	uniquely crafted/gifted/ meaningful tasks/ Him/to others
III-A:	deeper appreciation/ God-given gifts/abilities
III-B:	evaluate/clarity/confidence
III-C:	invaluable insights relationally
III-D:	new freedom/employ/ meaningful ways

SESSION 13

I-A:	unique design/come alive
I-B:	personal mission statement
I-C:	uniquely crafted/gifted/ meaningful tasks/Him/ to others
II-A:	made you
II-B:	opportunities
II-C:	relating better
II-D:	new freedom
III-A:	physical makeup
III-B:	perceptions
III-C:	styles of communication
III-D:	approaches to learning
III-D1:	form
IV-A:	a grace gift from God
IV-B:	conception/conversion

SESSION 14

I-A:	Function follows form
I-B1:	grace gift
I-B2:	conception/conversion
II-A1:	Turning away from self toward God/born again
II-A2:	A unique God-given ability that He uses to enrich and empower His original design in your life
II-B1:	sovereignty distributed by the Holy Spirit
II-B2:	given for the benefits of others
II-B3:	uniquely expressed with varied effects

III:	mutually exclusive/ complimentary

SESSION 15

I-B:	enrich/empower
I-B1:	sovereignly distributed
I-B2:	benefit of others
I-B3:	varied effects
I-C:	mutually exclusive/ complimentary
II-A1:	not limited/personality part/ unique combination
II-A2:	% bars/amounts of energy
II-A3:	greatest strengths/ foundation
II-A4:	attic/rely
II-A5:	personality structure
III-A Strengths:	Compassionate/sensitive/ warm
III-A Viewpoint:	Feelings
III-A Motivator:	person
III-A Population:	30/75/25
III-B Strengths:	Logical/organized/ responsible
III-B Viewpoints:	Thinking
III-B Motivator:	ideas/accomplishments
III-B Population:	25/25/75

SESSION 16

Harmonizer

I-B Strengths:	Compassionate/sensitive/ warm
I-B Viewpoints:	Feelings
I-B Motivator:	person

Achiever

I-B Strengths:	Logical/organized/ responsible
I-B Viewpoints:	Thinking
I-B Motivator:	ideas/accomplishments

Persister

II-A Strengths:	Dedicated/observant/ conscientious
II-A Viewpoint:	Evaluating
II-A Motivator:	convictions/beliefs
II-A Population:	10/25/75

Dreamer

II-B Strengths:	Imaginative/reflective/calm
II-B Viewpoint:	Reflecting
II-B Motivator:	private time/personal space
II-B Population:	10/60/40

Catalyzer

II-C Strengths:	Adaptable/persuasive/ charming
II-C Viewpoints:	Acting
II-C Motivator:	excitement/make things happen
II-C Population:	5/40/60

Energizer

II-D Strengths:	Spontaneous/creative/ playful
II-D Viewpoint:	Reacting
II-D Motivator:	playful contact/humor
II-D Population:	20/60/40

SESSION 17

I-A:	Harmonizer/feel/ Compassion
I-B:	Achiever/think/Logic
I-C:	Persister/evaluate/Values
I-D:	Dreamer/reflect/Imagination
I-E:	Catalyzer/act/Charm
I-F:	Energizer/react/Humor
I-Statement:	viewpoint/fluent in/ language/connect

SESSION 18

II-A:	mission statement/ slogan/word
II-B:	things/come alive
II-C:	yes/no/unique design/God
II-D:	spouse/design discovery
II-E:	proactive/finding your fit

II-F:	personal board/cheer/ accountable
II-G:	pursuits/Life Compass

SESSION 19

II-A:	defining moments/ be/pursuing/quits
II-B:	the high and noble
II-D:	is you/hills to climb/demons to face/battles to fight/raw faith and courage to go forward
II-E:	alone/Mama/wife/man
III-A:	time to reflect/your design/ your wiring and what tests "red"/your Life Compass
III-B:	safe people
III-C:	prioritized plan
III-D:	first things first

SESSION 20

I-A:	fight ... a good fight
II-A:	passivity
II-B:	doubt/what it takes/I believe ... really believe
III-A:	strongholds
III-B:	vision
III-C:	new ground
IV-A:	success
IV-B:	well lived/more to come

More Resources from Men's Fraternity

Imagine the transforming power of men coming together in your church to honestly examine their lives and to take the courageous steps necessary to embrace authentic biblical manhood.

That is the goal of Men's Fraternity, a powerful ministry created by Robert Lewis, pastor-at-large of Fellowship Bible Church in Little Rock, Arkansas.

Men's Fraternity is designed to foster true spiritual and emotional growth among men as they meet for weekly teaching sessions and small-group interaction. Each study is designed to engage the heart as well as the mind, stripping away the myths of manhood and focusing on how each individual can be transformed into a true man of God.

The Quest for Authentic Manhood

The original curriculum in the Men's Fraternity series, this 24-week study helps men understand their true identity and learn how to pursue genuine masculinity for a lifetime.

DVD SET
The 24 DVDs in this kit include teaching sessions by Robert Lewis, each with approximately 45 minutes of content. Church leaders can review his material and use it to create their own presentations or simply play the DVDs for the group.
001260518 • **$299.00**

VIEWER GUIDE
This workbook allows participants to easily follow along with presentations and provides a guide for later review. Also includes questions to help spur small-group discussion.
001260520 • **$9.95**

AUDIO CD PACK
Contains the audio portion of each session so that participants can review any sessions they miss.
001260519 • **$139.00**

Winning at Work & Home

As a man, are you looking for answers and seeking direction? This 16-week study will help you crack the code on what it means to be a real man. Discover how to win at work and at home, the two most critical areas of a man's life. Unlock the truth of authentic manhood and empower your everyday life!

DVD SET 001274717 • **$299.00**
VIEWER GUIDE 001274718 • **$9.95**
AUDIO CD PACK 001274719 • **$139.00**

Also from Robert Lewis

Raising a Modern-Day Knight Video Adventure Series

Based on the best-selling book, this six-part adventure series explores how dads can raise their sons into noble, vibrant masculinity and healthy manhood. Seven DVDs of instruction by Robert Lewis and Dennis Rainey, the book *Raising a Modern-Day Knight,* a leader guide, a training guide, and a legacy album equip men to connect with their sons and become effective and strategic fathers. For information or to purchase, visit *www.rmdk.com.*

TO ORDER OR FOR MORE INFORMATION,
call (800) 458-2772, visit *www.lifeway.com/mensfraternity,* or visit the LifeWay Christian Store serving you.